D1084673

L A
2 1
·S47

Democracy, Stoicism, and Education

An Essay in the History of Freedom and Reason

Robert R. Sherman

RITTER LIBRARY
BALDWIN-WALLACE COLLEGE
WITHDRAWN

University of Florida Press
Gainesville ● 1973

EDITORIAL COMMITTEE

Humanities Monographs

T. WALTER HERBERT, *Chairman*
Professor of English

J. WAYNE CONNER
Professor of Romance Languages
and Literatures

RICHARD H. HIERS
Professor of Religion

G. PAUL MOORE
Professor of Speech

CHARLES W. MORRIS
Professor Emeritus of Philosophy

REID POOLE
Professor of Music

C. A. ROBERTSON
Professor Emeritus of English

MELVIN E. VALK
Associate Professor of Germanic
Languages

Library of Congress Cataloging in Publication Data

Sherman, Robert R.   1930–
   Democracy, stoicism, and education.

   (University of Florida humanities monograph no. 40)
   Bibliography: p.
   1. Education—Philosophy.   2. Stoics.   3. Democracy.   I. Title.   II. Series:
Florida. University, Gainesville. University of Florida monographs.
Humanities, no. 40.
LA21.S47   370.1   73–6728
ISBN 0–8130–0391–1

COPYRIGHT©1973 BY THE STATE OF FLORIDA
BOARD OF TRUSTEES OF THE INTERNAL IMPROVEMENT TRUST FUND

PRINTED BY THE ROSE PRINTING COMPANY
TALLAHASSEE, FLORIDA

Preface

For a long time I have been interested in two forms of humanism—democracy and Stoicism. This study is an attempt to bring these theories together, through analysis, and to suggest some implications they have for education. In addition, if there can be gained from this study a better understanding of the democratic idea, an awareness that Stoicism had its rise in and provided a response to social and political circumstances similar to present realities, and thus some use of the Stoic philosophy to shed light on the ways in which democracy can respond better to the challenges in modern life, then I shall be satisfied.

The study began as a doctoral dissertation under the guidance of Professor James E. Wheeler of Rutgers University. Professor J. J. Chambliss, also of Rutgers University, gave me advice and encouragement. Professor Carlton H. Bowyer, now of Memphis State University, first encouraged me to study Stoicism. Many others have helped; they know who they are. I thank them all.

ROBERT R. SHERMAN

Contents

1
Freedom and Reason

SCHOLARS have noted consistently the debt that democratic theory owes to the Stoic philosophy. Sidney Hook, for example, writes that "ideologically, modern democratic theory owes more to Stoic philosophy and Roman law than to Christian dogma" ("The New Failure of Nerve," p. 92).* Ludwig Edelstein, a renowned classical scholar, said as recently as 1966 that Stoicism "still is . . . the political theory most dear to the hearts of all freedom-loving men" (p. 96). The purposes of this essay are to show, in part at least, the kind of ideological connection that exists between democratic theory and Stoicism, to suggest that both theories are educational in nature, and to set out some considerations for education which come from the Stoic thinkers.

It is quite common to suggest that democratic theory is educational in nature, and much has been written in the last century about democratic education. But very little about the Stoic philosophy may be called common knowledge, and not much is known about the import of that philosophy for education. Both democracy and Stoicism rest ultimately on a concept of "reason" which can be prescribed adequately only through an educational plan. Thus, in the Stoic system and in democracy there are relationships among freedom, reason, and education.

* Page numbers refer to works listed in the Bibliography.

1

At this point in history, however, reason is suspect and is the subject of much abuse and even dispraise. Perhaps because of the dominant influence of science despite its failure to cure all social ills, it has become fashionable to extoll the virtue of believing in and acting on faith instead of reason. A number of ready examples stand out. In religion, the faith of the Middle Ages, which appealed to reason for its justification, has given way to faith without reason. In philosophy, the Existential movement of recent years has been taken by some uncritical followers to indicate the failure of reason. Robert Olson notes, "A relatively large group of artists, writers, intellectuals, and others have given unstinting praise to the [existential] movement precisely because of what they take to be its irrationalism" (p. 64). More recently, there has been a move to discredit reason in political matters. Much of the thinking and rhetoric of the New Left in the United States has been aimed toward that point, if it does not take it directly. A letter to George F. Kennan is an example: "To calmly speak the language of sterile rationality while all about us people die absurdly is criminal. It is time for those who place their faith in the order of the rational mind to heed the call of the heart" (p. 53).

Strangely enough, those who deprecate reason do not usually at the same time denigrate freedom or education. Apparently their thinking is that freedom and education can exist even where reason is suspect. But this is wrong. Freedom in the Western world has been worked out through reason, through the use of intelligence. And education is an extension of reason: it is the systematic shaping of intelligence, so that no education worthy of the name could exist where there is suspicion of reason. An explication of the connection between democratic theory and Stoicism should show the extent to which reason, freedom, and education are related; and the explication has a modern use as well, as it is an interpretation of the history of an idea. It is better to work out these connections, and to note the educational import in detail, than it is to prescribe irrationality as the cure for the ills of society and as the new savior of freedom. A better use of reason, rather than its abandonment, may be found from the study of these connections.

This discussion is presented as a brief sketch. An effort is made to present a complete discussion, though not one embellished in great detail. Besides presenting the ideas and following their development, the citation of sources for the ideas should be valuable. In chapters 2 and 3, a general account is given of democratic theory and the Stoic philosophy, ideals, and methods, and a number of connections between those theories are described. This is the basis for the discussion in chapter 4 of explicit educational topics. The primary interest is in what the Stoics had to say about education and matters of educational import. Here frequent use is made of quotations from basic Stoic sources. The intent is to see what the Stoics themselves had to say about an education consistent with the philosophic and political theories described earlier.

The views described are intended as an essay in persuasion and appreciation. They are unique in the way in which parallels between democratic and Stoic theory are drawn and implications for education are stated. The views are intended mainly for a general humanities audience, particularly for those who come to know Stoicism—if at all—through English translations and commentaries, but can be useful specifically to students of philosophy of education. It should be understood that both Stoicism and democracy have had long histories, during which time the theories have been modified in a variety of ways. But the central principles of both theories have remained intact. It is because of this that the general discussion, especially the discussion of Stoic education, is presented as if the ideas came from the mind of one person instead of having traveled the long road of history to their current form.

2
Ideals

BOTH democracy and Stoicism are "ways of life." These systems of thought rest on the belief that the good life results from a concern with and an investigation into all the parts of life and that it is achieved through the interaction of ends and means, or ideals and methods. Democracy in the first instance is a political theory, primarily a method of government, and Stoicism is predominantly a moral philosophy or a moral ideal. But these systems are not restricted to politics or morals, nor are they, unlike a common opinion, merely a method of government on the one hand and a moral ideal on the other. Democracy also is a moral ideal; it is a vision (vague or sketchy at times, perhaps) of the kind of life worth living and how it can be lived, a vision to which the methods of government must be directed. And, although Stoicism is known primarily as a moral ideal, it, too, has a methodology for use in moving toward the ideal.

The moral ideal of Stoicism is "reason." The Stoics use other terms—virtue, happiness, goodness, knowledge—from time to time to refer to the moral ideal (D.L., vii. 135, 147),* but reason is used most often and it is the most suggestive term. Reason implies "intelligence," or the mind at work. The life of reason is the aim of every Stoic. But reason is more than an aim or goal. It is also the means by which the good life is achieved. That is, a life ruled

* See the Appendix for a key and note on the classical citations used in this essay.

5

by intelligence is not only an end to be sought, but it is through the mind at work that such a life is achieved. Thus, the Stoic ideal refers both to the ends and means of life. This should not be surprising. Stoicism is a unified system of philosophy which takes the order of nature as a pattern for its ideal. According to the Stoics, all things in nature are related; therefore, the parts of philosophy are related, too (D.L., vii. 39–40). The ends and means of life are joined together, and there is no essential difference between them. Ends and means have different functions, of course, and they may be separated for purposes of study, but they are equal and integrated parts of the whole system of philosophy. Because of this, the Stoics insist on such principles, for example, that speculation must lead to action—that is, the aim of theory is practice (e.g., Epictetus, *Man.* 46; M.A., x. 16)—and that men should follow reason in all things.

Democracy has a similar conception of ends and means which equally depend on reason. It is also the case that in democracy, theory must not be separated from practice, and the democrat must follow reason in all public deliberations. Again it should be clear that reason refers to intelligence. The good life, or democratic living, can be realized consciously, deliberately, and systematically only through the use of intelligence.

Not all critics agree that democracy implies a unity of ends and means, or ideals and methods, so it is necessary to construct the view. Lord Bryce, the well-known interpreter of democracy, says in one place that "democracy . . . is merely a form of government, not a consideration of purposes to which government may be turned" (p. 67). Perhaps skepticism over the conception and use of ideals leads many democrats to this opinion. Ideals of democracy in the past often have been vague, merely symbolic, or narrowly conceived as a particular truth or good. While there is a sense in which vagueness can be useful, such as that noted by John Dewey (p. 104), in which a tentative sketch often serves to direct inquiry satisfactorily, surely one would be wise to reject vague democratic ideals if they did not direct the democratic process adequately. Also, ideals that merely proclaim virtue but which have no function in directing democratic action should also be rejected. And when democratic ideals are too narrowly conceived, such as when property, wealth, or status are taken as the ends of life, the democrat has reason to reject them, for such ideals are used often to justify an undemocratic methodology.

For these reasons, it is not surprising that some persons do believe that it makes better sense to consider democracy as a process or a means of government and not as an ideal. Going beyond Bryce, a representative of this view, Ernest Bayles, says that "whenever we define democracy in terms of product [e.g., ideals] rather than of process, we defeat the very end we are seeking" (p. 152). Democracy is not an end to be gained, only a means or a method for determining those ends. Democracy is the process of popular sovereignty, and the popular will is determined by majority rule. Thus, Bayles says, "If a people's will is not to be taken, for a given occasion, as final, then we do not have democracy . . ." (p. 162).

Certainly popular sovereignty is what democracy is about, and majority rule is accepted universally as part of the process through which the popular will is determined. But the notion that democracy can do without ideals creates its own problems. What happens if the majority takes an action to foreclose on the entire community—if, for instance, it terminates the existing form of government or if it makes unreasonable restrictions in the franchise? The critic of ideals might be inclined to argue, as Bayles does, that "we might democratically decide to eliminate democracy entirely," and that "it could be democratic for a majority to hold a group disenfranchised because of skin color or sex" (pp. 158, 162). But one who thinks in this manner fails to understand that a process must have a direction if it is not to yield, willy-nilly, products—thought and action—that are as often as debilitating or destructive to democracy as they are helpful. In the haste to cast off misconceived ideals, the democratic process is left with no sense of direction, and consequently it is used to deduce and justify actions that offend the democratic intent—continued and equal popular sovereignty. Boyd Bode noted this tendency in 1939, and he made it clear that democracy must be considered in some sense as an ideal: "The rise of dictatorships is creating an uneasy and inarticulate sense that democracy symbolizes an as yet undefined ideal or principle of social organization and is not to be identified altogether with method" ("Ends and Means," p. 13).

Democracy needs the regulation or sense of direction that ideals provide, as well as the freedom of speculation and experimentation that is the process of life. These elements work together in a democracy; each regulates and helps fulfill the other. For this reason, democratic ideals may be said to be "regulative" ideals (cf. Hook, *The Hero in History*, pp. 239–41), and as such they are to be distinguished from the misconceived ideals mentioned before. Also, they are to be distinguished from metaphysical ideals (e.g., ideals in the Platonic sense). The regulative ideals of democracy are general outlines of the direction in which democracy must move. They are drawn from experience; they are used to organize, direct, and regulate the democratic process; and they are flexible, that is, in their particular formulations they are used only insofar as they direct the democratic process adequately and are reformulated when they do not. In a real sense, regulative ideals are the life-blood of democracy, for they set the conditions necessary to maintain the democratic process.

A number of regulative ideals may be stated for democracy, but a review of one should make the point. Democracy is committed to the general regulative ideal of "openness"; that is, the democratic process is regulated or guided by it. Openness is an often stated ideal of democracy, sometimes explicitly, as when a democratic society is called an "open society," sometimes implied in a description of democracy, such as that given by Daniel Boorstin. He notes that the essential commitment of American democracy (if there is any point in talking about "essential commitments") is not to a collection of ideological idols but to a body of rules that keeps the ideological temple empty (p. 170).

Even though it is commonly expressed, the meaning of openness is not always understood or appreciated. In its essential respects, openness implies that democracy must be protected as a continuous process. Thus, actions that result in restricting, or closing off, or terminating the democratic process (other than temporarily) cannot be democratic. The regulative ideal of openness implies, rather, that the results of the democratic process must lead to a continued opportunity for democratic participation. It is because of this that the termination of democracy by a majority and the disfranchisement of a group on the basis of sex or race, if permanent arrangements, are inconsistent with the democratic idea of popular sovereignty.

The regulative ideal of openness may be called a rational ideal. Democracies have been justified throughout history on the basis of such an ideal, usually called "natural law." From its origin with the early Greeks, through its central formulation by the Stoics—best expressed by Cicero (*Rep.*

iii. 22)—to its use in the seventeenth and eighteenth centuries to justify democratic revolutions, natural law has been used as an objective moral standard to determine and measure human ideas, actions, and institutions. It is the standard of reason.

There is no need to follow through the centuries various quarrels about the natural law (e.g., does such a moral principle exist objectively? are its claims absolute, unchanging, and unerring?) in order to agree that the theory still has use as a regulative ideal. The theory implies at least the recommendation that reason is to be followed in the conduct of democratic affairs. Neither is it necessary to quarrel over whether or not natural law expressions state the quality and conditions of life as they really are. What profit is there, for example, in trying to settle the argument of whether "all men are created equal," as the American Declaration of Independence insists, and whether that equality is biological as well as political, social as well as educational? The ideal is intended to describe what life can and should be—it is an aspiration and a plan of action. The good life is achieved through the use of intelligence.

For democratic politics, openness also implies more specific things. Basically, it is a requirement that democratic theory and practice must be subject to review and change; for example, legislation must be subject to amendment. The ideal implies also that the opportunity to engage in the democratic process must not be limited unreasonably. It is the intent of democracy to encourage all persons to be a part of their own self-government, and varieties of evidence necessary for intelligent decision-making must be available to all who are involved in the process. This means in practice that the democratic process is public, pluralistic, and empirical. The ideal of openness may be understood from a variety of perspectives: it may be called the principle

of review, the principle of social change, or the principle
of continued intelligence. All of these suggest two primary
qualities of democratic ideals: flexibility and regulation.
Thus, when the political scientist William Ebenstein says,
"Democracy may be defined as the right to make mistakes"
(p. 142), an awareness of the idea of openness should make
such a definition clear and understandable.

All of this implies that the democratic ideal of reason or openness is a scientific ideal; that is, the ideal is a
political expression of a more general intellectual ideal, one
noted most clearly and most often, perhaps, in scientific
thinking. It is the ideal of continued intelligence. Charles
Sanders Peirce has given a fine statement of this ideal as
the first (primary) rule of reason. He says that in order
to learn, one must desire to do so and must not be content
with what is already known; from this follows the corollary
"Do not block the way of inquiry" (p. 54). For democracy,
as for other intellectual pursuits, this implies specifically
that politics is not a system of absolutes and that it does
not seek perfection; that plural claims to knowledge and
truth are legitimate and even necessary to the democratic
process; that the products of the democratic process are
fallible, corrigible, tentative, and never certain; and that
the final test of the democratic process is whether or not
it leads to a greater opportunity to employ that process
in the life of man.

It is in this sense that certain descriptions of democracy,
such as the following from H. Gordon Hullfish, show the
general intellectual connection between the rule of reason
in science and in politics. He says, "Democracy is no com-
pleted product which may be reflected in . . . any institution
of a free culture. Insofar as men achieve it in any measure
. . . they simply deepen their understanding of how to
aspire to greater achievement. There is no end to this road"

(p. v). The ideal of reason—openness—implies that the good life for democracy is not perfection but rather a method to be used for continuous improvement.

Stoicism has a similar view of ideals. That its ideal is reason, and that the ideal denotes a unity of ends and means, has been mentioned. Like democracy, Stoicism is a theory of action. Throughout history, Stoics counseled that action is the real end of thought. Marcus Aurelius, the Roman Stoic and emperor, expresses this counsel well when he says, "Don't any more discuss at large what the good man is like, but be good" (x. 16). Action, however, must be directed toward appropriate ends, so that ideals are necessary. Like the democrat, the Stoic draws his ideals from experience. The ideal of the wise man is a good example: the Stoics draw on existing stories and the lives of wise men, both mythical and historical, to teach virtue. Hercules is the best of their models, as he was a model for all Greece, mainly because he labored for the good of all men (Cicero, *Off*. iii. 5; Epictetus, *Disc*. iii. 24. 13). Others, such as Ulysses, various wise and prudent kings, and philosophers (many of them now portrayed in the *Lives* of Diogenes Laertius), are used also as examples of virtue. Socrates, Diogenes (the Cynic), Heraclitus, Cleanthes, and Zeno (of Citium) are examples used by the early Stoics; among the Romans, the lives of Marcus Cato (the Younger), Epictetus, and Marcus Aurelius are examples of the Stoic ideal.

Though the Stoics have been thought to be "rationalists" in the Platonic sense (that mind and its products, not experience, is real), their ideals, always based on experience, suggest that this is not so. They do, of course, believe in "inborn ideas," which are principles that direct the mind toward absolute and perfect knowledge (Epictetus, *Disc*. ii. 11. 2–4). These principles, however, are not Platonic; according to Arnold, they are only "rough outlines" that depend on experience for their being and on the exercise of reason for their development. (pp. 137–38). The Stoics are rationalists, not in the Platonic sense, but in their belief that intelligence always is necessary to organize experience and to gain perspective from experience. Their ideals thus are a combination of experience and reason.

The Stoic ideal has been criticized from time to time as unattainable. Perhaps this criticism is based on the fact that the Stoics give no evidence that anyone ever has become fully rational or wise. Cicero notes that the Stoics believe no one has achieved the ideal (*Orat.* iii. 18). But surely ideals that are soundly conceived in experience must be attainable in some measure. Unattainable ideals are as much of an anathema for the Stoic as they are for the democrat. To note this, one may turn again to an observation made so often in connection with the Stoic system: that speculation removed from life is a violation of philosophy. Some men have come close to the ideal. Epictetus remarks that "Diogenes and Heraclitus, and men like them, were deservedly divine and deservedly so called," for they knew how to act appropriately (*Man.* 15). Also, he says, "This is the way Socrates became what he was, by paying attention to nothing but his reason in everything that he encountered" (*Man.* 51).

That no one has attained the theoretical ideal, an abstract image of perfection, should not cause skepticism, for the real function of the ideal, a practical function, is to draw one on to continuous improvement. Marcus Aurelius cautions men not to "hope for Plato's Utopia, but be content to make a very small step forward and reflect that the result even of this is no trifle" (ix. 29). The ideal should stimulate improvement and progress, even if perfection cannot be attained. In this sense the ideal has a regulative purpose and function like democratic ideals. Epictetus counsels,

"Even if you are not yet a Socrates, still you ought to live as one who wishes to be a Socrates" (*Man.* 51). Later Stoics accept progress, rather than perfection, as the ideal of virtue. "The proof," says Posidonius, "that virtue really exists is the fact that Socrates, Diogenes, and Antisthenes and their followers made moral progress" (D.L. vii. 91).

Yet the notion that the Stoic ideal is unattainable persists and gives support to another common belief, that they were absolutists. Hijmans' view of Epictetus as an absolutist and a dogmatist is but one example of this belief (pp. 21–22). In order to evaluate the belief for the Stoics in general, it must be noted that Stoicism has two parts: a theoretical system, in which absolute reason is idealized, and a practical or general system, which is used in the conduct of the common affairs of life, as a guide for progress toward the ideal (cf. Christensen). In theory, the Stoic aims for certainty, which is absolute reason, knowledge, or truth. This aim corresponds to the ideal of modern science which strives for complete and perfect knowledge. But there is no reason to believe that certainty ever is achieved in human affairs—no more so in Stoicism than in science or democratic politics—so a practical ideal is formulated.

The practical ideal is described as a part of the Stoic method; an example is the Stoic use of natural law theory. While original formulations of an absolute natural law of reason come from the Stoic system, the theory develops in its practical applications not as a metaphysical abstraction but as the idea of "consensus," or the standard of the agreement of rational men. All forms of liberalism, democracy no less than Stoicism, undergo a similar development. W.D. Grampp notes, "As liberalism developed in detail, particularly in its economic aspects, it moved away from natural law doctrine and fixed upon the idea of consensus. This was also the course of Stoicism" (p. 147). Thus, in practice (which is what counts in life), the Stoics shun the absolute and act instead on the relative basis of experience and consensus.

The practical ideal of the Stoic is, then, a flexible one. Reason has various forms; it can grow or be diminished, and its material import at a particular time depends on experience. In practice the Stoics are not metaphysicians, nor are they absolutists or dogmatists. They are not disposed to accept or assert principles of knowledge without critical evaluation, without drawing those principles from experience, and without leaving room for doubt. (Hijmans has called Epictetus a dogmatist, but he does agree [p. 22] that self-criticism has an important role even in Epictetus' thought.) Epictetus says in a memorable passage in the *Discourses* that the first business of philosophy is "to get rid of thinking that one knows; for it is impossible to get a man to begin to learn that which he thinks he knows" (ii. 17. 1). This is a dramatic expression of the ideal of openness. One must not block the way of inquiry. Seneca provides other examples. Richard M. Gummere has described him as "a pluralist at heart, like William James; he could tolerate no generalities which were irrevocable, but made up his world from his own personal investigations and ideas" (p. 50). In his words, Seneca says he shall follow his predecessors, but if necessary he will open a new road, for all truth has not been discovered (*Epis.* 33. 11).

The Stoic ideal also is a regulative ideal. It is an image designed to attract one to the life of reason and to regulate the process of reason. Reason, or intelligence, is a practical guide for life. The ideal comes from experience; it is flexible; and its primary purpose, in leading to the good life, is to maintain the process of reason. Thus, for the Stoic the primary commitment in life is to the process of reason, and there is no proximate end to this process. Ludwig Edelstein remarks about the Stoic ideal, "For the Stoic there is no real aim of [the] rational process, no real end. The Stoics are not unclear about what reason wants: their reason wants nothing but realization. Certainly there are relative purposes. . . . But all [of these purposes are] true only within the process of growth. There is no overall purpose or aim; the realization of the inherent force is the end or purpose itself, and this realization is the only value to be realized" (pp. 32–33). When the Stoic says that virtue should be chosen for its own sake, or suggests that virtue is its own reward (D.L., vii. 127; Cicero, *Fin.* iii. 38–39), the implication is clear, in the same way that it is for the democrat, that the primary result of free thought and action must be to open life and to extend and deepen its meaning.

Are the Stoics committed fully to such an ideal? In a sense one asks if they are committed fully to the scientific attitude (of which openness is a part) and to the implications of scientific analysis. Particularly, do the Stoics believe that scientific investigation is a natural and effective procedure for the discovery and interpretation of knowledge, that the procedure is self-corrective, and that it is guided by the twin ideals of truth and openness? The preceding discussion is intended to show that in its practical teachings and applications Stoicism has a characteristically scientific attitude. According to the Stoics, the basis of all knowledge is empirical; experience is interpreted through the method of reason; and the attitude of the open mind implies, in part, a self-corrective principle.

Insofar as their teaching can be judged, one may even say the Stoics are inclined to be experimental. Proximate aims, their teaching, and their counsel, are to be used as hypotheses for directing life. This counsel has to be tested in life—it has to be put to use and judged for its worth. Seneca implies such a thing many times in his *Epistles* (e.g.,

33. 11; 45. 4), especially when he says that the discoveries of the past are not our masters but our guides. Epictetus gives a similar counsel. To a person who was displaying his knowledge of what wise men said, Epictetus asks, "Where do you get that knowledge? . . . Have you . . . tested any of these statements and have you formed your own judgement upon them?" (*Disc.* ii. 19. 14).

Some interpretations, however, suggest that Stoicism is antiscientific. W. W. Tarn says that "the weakness of Stoicism was its detachment from the scientific spirit" (p. 312), and Eduard Zeller criticizes what he considers to be the Stoic rejection of the ideal of pure science and intellectual creation (pp. 402–3). Gilbert Murray implies that the Stoics were not basically scientific: "One may . . . notice that in [the Peripatetic] school alone it is assumed as natural that further research will take place and will probably correct as well as increase our knowledge, and that, when such corrections or differences of opinion do take place, there is no cry raised of Heresy" (*Five Stages*, p. 111). He notes that the gradual abatement in the ancient world of interest in truth for its own sake was "the old difference between Philosophy and Religion, between the search of the intellect for truth and the cry of the heart for salvation" (ibid., p. 112).

Paradoxically, though, Murray does not say that Stoicism abandoned the ideal of intellect. In fact, after the intellectual example of Aristotle was forgotten, "the Porch [Stoicism] and the Garden [Epicureanism], for the most part, divided between them the allegiance of thoughtful men" (*Five Stages*, p. 112). But was this attraction for thoughtful men the scientific ideal? One must believe that Stoicism was a philosophy, not a religion—that it was rational sight, not faith—and that it was an approach to truth instead of truth itself, if it is to be judged so.

Perhaps those who consider Stoicism to be antiscientific attend too much to particular theories that one Stoic or another held or to a misunderstanding of the scientific attitude. The beliefs of Tarn and Zeller seem to be of this kind. Tarn thought that Stoicism was unscientific mainly because some of its adherents believed in astrology. Zeller probably thought that because the Stoics emphasize the utility of intellect and the practicality of philosophy, they must necessarily reject pure science and intellectual creation (as some Stoics may have done in fact). These notions, however, are not well founded. Particular points of view and the idea of utility are not enough in themselves to determine an antiscientific attitude. Such an attitude must be determined by noting the assumptions one holds, the method to which one is committed in the search for knowledge, and the effort given to that search.

The scientific attitude is marked by three characteristics: the assumptions that truth can be known, but that one must hold an open mind for further discovery; a method that is empirical, rational, and experimental; and an idea of human effort that is public and collective. The Stoics act on each of these bases. Moreover, as Cicero notes, they understand clearly that morality must be determined by intent and effort, by judging purpose and action, not results (*Fin.* iii. 32). Results can be useful in determining whether or not intent and effort are rational, that is, if intent is good and effort is well directed, but rationality (the moral life) is essentially a method and not a particular belief, program, or set of answers. Another scientific assumption is that, if employed correctly, the attitude and method described as scientific will yield more than any other method more useful claims to knowledge, and thus lead more directly and expeditiously to the good life. Perhaps this can be called a "faith" (that is, a trust) in science. The

Stoic faith in reason is a similar kind of trust. It is surprising that some criticism of Stoicism (e.g., Hijmans, pp. 21–22) does not recognize this rational trust, but sees the system instead as closed, dogmatic, and thus antiscientific.

A man, or even a consensus of men, may have mistaken beliefs and still be scientific, for the adjective "scientific" indicates the process used to develop ideas, not the ideas themselves. Faulty ideas may stem from misinformation, or the use of different assumptions, or they may be erroneous only when judged at a different time and under different circumstances. According to some Stoics, the belief in astrology is rational. As early as the fifth and fourth centuries B.C., it had been established through research in mathematics, astronomy, and biology that there is an inherent law and order in the universe, and astrology was useful in understanding and demonstrating this law and order. Other Stoics, such as Cleanthes and even Posidonius, the foremost scientist of the second century B.C., were aware of the heliocentric theory, but, as Arnold (pp. 178–79) and Edelstein (p. 30) note, they reject that theory in their own philosophy because it clashes with the logic of other studies such as metaphysics and theology. But they need not be branded as irrational or antiscientific for this. Edelstein (p. 30) remembers the need for caution in evaluating such matters when he recalls that Francis Bacon rejected the Copernican system and that Plato and Aristotle chose any theory of the universe they thought agreed with their ideas of philosophical truth.

Neither is there an inconsistency between the ideals of pure science and intellectual creation, or (more generally) the ideal of truth, and the belief that philosophy is useful and must have practical results. An ideal is an end, and utility involves means to an end, but ends and means, as the Stoics note, are joined in life. It follows from this, as well as from the Stoic beliefs that philosophy is practical and that virtue is its own reward, that truth has utility and that if a thing is useful it will lead to truth. Perhaps it is a prejudice of some classicists to dichotomize between truth as an ideal and the utility of truth. This prejudice, however, is neither in accord with the common purposes of nearly all of ancient philosophy, nor a necessary part of the scientific attitude. The Stoics are highly interested in truth for its own sake, that is, they are interested in the ideals of pure science and intellectual creation; but the purpose (the "sake") of truth is to be a guide toward the good life.

From this, it is more to the point to conclude that the Stoics are scientific. This is true especially if Stoics of the middle period, significantly Panaetius and Posidonius, are judged for their scientific work and their inclination toward the scientific attitude. Other Stoics before and after them (Epictetus is a good example) are not inclined to emphasize scientific study, either abstract theory or the physical sciences, perhaps because their primary interest is in moral theory and education. But under the influence of Panaetius and Posidonius, the original absolute system of ethics is tempered by practical considerations that give rise to a more scientific approach to knowledge and morality. The sciences, natural studies in general and even some human sciences such as history, reach a point of high order and systematic development during the middle period of Stoicism. According to Edelstein, it is then that "that science was created to which modern science at the beginning of the Renaissance harked back" (pp. 49–50). There is a greater interest in factual knowledge rather than speculation, and rational investigation comes to replace the inchoate empiricism and experiments of earlier times.

The influence for much of this can be traced to

Posidonius. But more importantly, Posidonius believes, even more so than Aristotle, Edelstein claims, thet the search for knowledge is a "continual progress, in which no generation reaches the final end" (pp. 66–67). This view is evident also in the writings of Epictetus and Seneca. Thus, science, Stoicism, and democracy all are guided by a common ideal—openness. One must keep an open mind in the search for truth, or the good life, for toward this end there is always something new to be discovered. In the new discoveries is contained the progress necessary to make the good life more of a reality for Stoics as well as democrats.

Stoicism is a form of humanism. It has been said, by Edelstein, in fact, that Stoicism is the foundation of all later forms of humanism (p. 42). The continuous use of Stoic ideals and insights throughout history validates this opinion. The philosophy begins in troubled times and thrives most when life is at its lowest ebb—from the Peloponnesian Wars, through the wars of Alexander, to the defeat of Greece by Rome in 146 B.C. The Stoics seek to provide a new way to deal with change and the chaos and despair that so often accompany it. Ancient laws and traditions and personal habits are ineffective and thus irrelevant for the new times, and the mystical and transempirical basis of much of life, especially religion and politics, no longer provides a satisfactory foundation for life. Stoicism turns to man himself for the solution. It centers on distinctively human interests and ideals and teaches that man can make his own way through the use of reason. This humanistic ideal, begun by Zeno and his followers, was exalted years later by the Romans as *humanitas*, a common bond of reason uniting men and society. In Rome, the faith in man's ability to conduct his own affairs intelligently almost takes on the proportions of a new religion.

The Stoic humanistic ideal rises again in the sixteenth century. It is embodied mostly in literature, but leads in some cases to a study of Stoic ethics and a concern with making those ethics compatible with Christianity. Man is exalted as a natural being who needed only to exercise his natural capacities to make his own greatness.

Today, the humanistic ideal is most nearly embodied in democratic theory. Is this perhaps a surprising assertion? Some critics might observe that it is a strange form of humanism that substitutes, as democracy does, compromise and consensus for truth, that makes a virtue of utility, that glorifies what appears to be the mediocrity of the masses and subordinates the superior intellect and education of the relatively few. The strangeness, however, is in the point of view that would set compromise and consensus, utility, and the mind of the many in opposition to the classical ideal of humanism, for these things characterize the ideal and method, and thus the humanism, of Stoicism. Humanism is based on the one characteristic that men, *all* men, have in common: reason. Surely there is no opposition between humanism and the democratic belief that all men can and should control and conduct their own affairs and that they should be guided by reason in this task. The beliefs are in fact identical.

Neither is there a contradiction between humanism and the democratic method of compromise and consensus (which are discussed in more detail later). To the contrary, these, too, are identical, for compromise and consensus are methods that have been used since the time of the Stoics to make rational agreement the basis of conduct. Consensus, the agreement of rational men, comes from the Roman idea of natural law, which has its beginnings in Stoic theory and which has found its way into democratic theory and survives today as one of the bases for democratic rule. Furthermore, utility need not be deprecated if one is to follow humanistic principles in modern life. It has been noted that the Stoic philosophers, and the Greeks in general, have no argument against the utility that philosophy can serve. In fact, philosophy, or political theory, or theory of any kind, that has no utility is considered to be a waste of time.

Some persons probably deny that democracy is a form of humanism because in its theory and practice it rejects metaphysics. Leo Strauss is a critic of this type. He believes, for example, that Americans generally accept the principles of the Declaration of Independence as ideals rather than as "self-evident, objective, natural rights"; and this view, he proposes, is identical with nihilism (pp. 1–5). On the other hand, at least one critic, H. J. Blackham, denies that Stoicism is humanism because it *does* profess a metaphysics, a belief in an objective law of reason (p. 127). This is a contradiction that can be resolved only by insisting that metaphysics need not be and in fact is not the test of humanism. The matter depends on what relation the metaphysical has to the practical life. The test of humanism is how man looks at himself and what responsibility he takes for shaping his life. Blackham says, "Humanism proceeds from an assumption that man is on his own and this life is all and an assumption of responsibility for one's own life and for the life of mankind—an appraisal and an undertaking, two personal decisions. Less than this is never humanism" (p. 13).

Both democracy and Stoicism meet this test of humanism, that is, both begin with these assumptions about man. And both go beyond the assumptions to prescribe a framework for the humanistic undertaking. Democracy provides a political framework for making the humanistic ideal operative, and the Stoic logical and epistemological methods have strik-

ing similarities to that framework. Stoicism certainly
appears to go even *beyond* this (note that Blackham says
it must not be *less*) to believe in a god of reason who sustains
the universe. But the point is that in practice the Stoic
looks only to himself for the principles of action and, employ-
ing intelligence, works himself to determine his own life.
It is in this sense that Stoicism and democracy are forms
of humanism.

The humanism of democracy and Stoicism may be judged
in another way. In doing so, it must be remembered that
humanism is both an appraisal and an undertaking of life.
According to Paul Tillich, Stoicism and democracy are each
courageous undertakings, but there is a difference between
Stoic and democratic courage: the Stoic faces catastrophe
with the courage of resignation, turning away from the
world, while the democrat has the courage to work for
new foundations (pp. 107–8). It is a fact that the Stoics
both preach and practice resignation, which is an acceptance
of fate. This is called "apathy" by the Stoics, or an indiffer-
ence to the passions (D.L. vii. 117). On the other hand,
the democrat certainly is not inclined to turn away from
the world. He shows not only a courage to work for new
foundations, to change the world, but even an enthusiasm
to get on with the work. Tillich's view is typical in its
implication that the Stoics do not work positively to bring
about a new intellectual, moral, political, and social order.
That is, the common thought is that the Stoics do not
care for political and social action. If this is so, it would
be difficult to show how the Stoics were humanists and
how their political theory is the ideal of freedom-loving
men.

It is not so, however. The Stoics teach explicitly that
political and social activities are natural, that they can contribute to the good life, and therefore are a part of man's

duty (D.L. vii. 121, 123). Cicero, a critic of their ethics, admits that the Stoics know that men must engage in politics and government (*Fin.* iii. 68). Stoics themselves actually engaged in political and social activities whenever they saw it to be in their interest and in the interest of mankind. Many were influential in governing Greece and Rome. Zeno was the friend and confidant of Antigonus Gonatas, the Macedonian king; Sphaerus, an advisor to King Cleomenes III of Sparta; Panaetius and Posidonius influenced the political affairs of Rome through their association with the Scipionic Circle; Seneca, prime minister in the reign of Nero; and Marcus Aurelius, the last Stoic of antiquity, a king in his own right.

In view of this, the Stoic idea of resignation cannot mean that men should not work positively for a better life. Resignation really reflects the Stoic idea that men must not attempt to deal with life on the basis of the passions or emotions. Rather, reason is the proper guide for life. External forces must be accepted for whatever they are. If they can be directed by reason, things may change for the better; if they cannot be so directed, one should not cling to them at any cost, but should let them loose and resign himself to live with the better consequences of withdrawal. The life of Marcus Cato is a good example of the Stoic view. Cato believes that it is proper for men to engage in politics, and he does so himself; but before his death he forbids his son to do the same thing, for "to do so worthily of a Cato was no longer possible, as things were going, and to do so otherwise would be disgraceful" (Plutarch, *Cato* 66. 3).

Stoic resignation, in its intent and practice, does not contradict the activist spirit, or the courage, of democracy. (Modern critics of politics and society who turn to Stoicism to justify withdrawal from life would do better to take their models from the Cynics and Epicureans.) In several of its implications, resignation is consistent with an active democratic theory. First, as noted, it is the determination to be guided by intelligence, not emotion; and it leads to withdrawal only when no other plan of action works. For another thing, it shows (in yet another way) that Stoicism is not a system of absolutes. Though it is natural and is man's duty to engage in worldly affairs, engagement is not an obligation. Sometimes engagement is not in man's best interest. Such occasions can be determined intelligently, and when they occur, resignation is a rational alternative.

The point is that no particular action has an absolute claim as duty. The single important duty (and this is true for democracy as well as for Stoicism) is to follow the process of reason in determining appropriate actions. Also, resignation implies that reason must focus on the facts of life as they exist. It does no good to hope for another set of circumstances in which life is easier or for which others are responsible. One must be resigned to what happens, that is, one must work within the existing situation and try through reason to fashion a satisfactory basis for living. In these ways, Stoic courage is not different from democratic courage. The Stoics do in fact propose and practice a type of courage to work for new foundations, through reason and based on empirical fact.

3

Methods

DEMOCRACY and Stoicism also have methods or set forms of procedure for determining specific policies to be followed in progress toward the ideal or the good life. The preceding discussion of ideals is not intended to deny this but to show that a "vision of the ends of life" is necessary even for theories that are considered most often to be political. Specifically, this is the case with democracy. On the other hand, Stoicism, most often thought to be only an ideal, also has a method to be used in approaching its ideal. One should conclude from this discussion that all well-developed political and social philosophies, ancient and modern, have both ideals and methods. Methods are as necessary for achieving ideals as ideals are necessary for directing the process of life adequately. A comment from Seneca illustrates this point: "We must set before our eyes the goal of the Supreme Good, towards which we may strive, and to which all our acts and words may have reference—just as sailors must guide their course according to a certain star. Life without ideals is erratic: as soon as an ideal is to be set up, doctrines begin to be necessary" (*Epis.* 95. 45–46).

"Reason" (stated in one form or another) is the ideal of democracy and Stoicism. But reason does not represent only the direction toward which these systems work; it implies as well a plan or method for achieving that end. Such a plan is to use reason (intelligence) as a general empiri-

cal principle or rule for determining the particular ends
and means of life. The notion of general empirical rules
is used most often in the physical sciences, but it is appli-
cable also to the social sciences. The idea begins with the
view that there are in the physical world natural patterns
of behavior toward certain ends which can be observed
and described through general rules or laws. These rules
are used to guide further investigation and activity. The
rules are not perfect, but are subject to amendment
whenever additional evidence is discovered and whenever
different insights suggest more fruitful explorations. Reason
thus is used basically to trace a general outline for action.
Social matters follow a similar pattern. The ends or ideals
of life can be attained by following a pattern of behavior
determined by reason. This pattern may change from time
to time, and no doubt it will differ in details and application
from one situation to another, but the basic pattern may
be stated as a general rule to be used in working toward
democratic and Stoic ends.

"Methods" must not be confused here with the day-to-day
operations of a political system. The concern here is not
with the routine through which a legislature or a committee
finally settles on a law or policy, e.g., priority of consideration, time limits for discussion, forms of enactment,
policies for voting, and so on. What is of interest is the
general intellectual procedure by which public policy is
determined and morality is judged. (One speaks specifically
of democracy in connection with public policy, but the
general intellectual procedure used by the Stoics to determine "truth" is similar. On the other hand, moral judgment,
which is the purpose of the Stoic search for truth, is equally
a democratic interest, for the determination of public policy
is the democratic morality.) In a democracy, it is generally
accepted that men do not have to agree on ultimate or

fundamental beliefs or on a particular form of truth or goodness, but they must agree, if they are to survive and thrive socially, on a method for determining what is true and how the good is to be tested. The study of method, then, is one in which the procedures and habits of mind necessary to promote the ideal of reason or openness are investigated.

Four possible ways of determining public policy and action may be analyzed in connection with the democratic methodology: unanimity, persuasion, force, and compromise. Each has been proposed at one time or another as legitimate and even basic to democracy. Whether or not these ways are essentially democratic and whether or not they are practical, which a method (especially the democratic and Stoic methods) must be if it is to direct action, are matters to be determined.

Unanimity, or universal agreement, implies that proposals for public policy and action must be agreeable to everyone or they should not be followed. For example, in the United States today there are many who believe that unless everyone agrees to a certain course of action, that action should not be instituted as public policy. Such a view has been heard most recently in matters relating to the racial desegregation of public facilities and the Supreme Court decisions about prayer in the public schools. Unanimity, however, is so impractical that it is hopeless to recommend it as a basis for action. All men do not agree, which is why a method for formulating agreements is necessary. To withhold action until they do agree is to insure either that no action will be taken or that whatever action is taken will be trivial.

Persuasion, another recommended method, ordinarily refers to the act of influencing another person through the use of rational arguments. Often, however, persuasion is associated with a metaphysical theory of truth and a belief that the purpose of democracy is to pursue that truth. (The article by Oliver Martin listed in the bibliography is an example.) One conclusion that should be drawn from the discussion of democratic ideals is that democracy is not a metaphysical theory and it does not pursue a metaphysical truth. The democratic method is used to formulate acceptable and workable policies for the time being. (This is the sense of democratic characteristics mentioned earlier; for example, "acceptable" implies "popular sovereignty," "workable" implies "practicality," and "for the time being" implies "openness.") Henry Mayo notes that democracy "is not designed to pursue truth, but to arrive at rightful and acceptable political decisions for the time being" (p. 235). Consequently, a metaphysical conception of persuasion cannot be part of the democratic method. For democracy, persuasion is not a general method; it is a technique, and just one aspect of method. Persuasion is that part of method that involves rational influence. Democrats try to influence each other through rational arguments, but this influence is but part of a more general democratic method.

Another suggested method is force, which is basically an appeal to physical strength. As such, it is authoritarian. Force is used to determine policies without reference to the free will and intelligence of the people. For this reason, it is not the method of democracy. Men always have been aware of the limitations of force. In the early days of Stoicism, the Cynic philosopher Crates tried to drag Zeno from the influence of Stilpo, another philosopher; but Zeno cautioned Crates that the proper way to seize a philosopher is by reason, for if force is used, "my body will be with you, but my mind with Stilpo" (D.L. vii. 24). Force must be used sparingly, if at all, in a democratic society. This is not to suggest that force has no role or will never be used in a democracy. It might be needed to remove certain obstructions to democracy, or to restore democracy, or to protect the survival of democracy. Certain wars and revolutions in history provide examples. But these are temporary and limited uses. A continuous use of force, where it is unrelated to the maintenance of democracy, cannot be recommended as the democratic method.

A similar point can be made for unanimity and persuasion. There may be occasions in a democracy where each of these plays a limited role. This is certainly true where persuasion and unanimity might be taken as rational ideals. For instance, Yves Simon says that "persuasion . . . would be the only instrument of government in a society of ideally perfect people" (p. 23). Unanimity might be a sensible ideal to follow at times, especially in matters that carry a consequence of life or death, such as a jury finding in a capital case, or in some things that affect the harmony of a limited group, such as the selection of an orchestra to play at a high school dance or a family decision about where to spend a vacation. Generally, though, unanimity, persuasion, and force do not state the basic characteristic of democratic method.

Compromise is the democratic method. It is a practical, general method for determining policy and action and for settling issues. From the earliest days of democracy, as far back as Greek times, compromise has been understood to be the only real alternative to force and the tragedy that results from the use of force. The plot of Sophocles' *Antigone* is an excellent example of the issue: when two people, believing they are right, oppose each other, what is the alternative to tragedy? Walter Agard suggests that the answer lies in the democratic principle of reasonable discussion and mutual concession, that is, compromise (p. 133). In democracy, compromise is used to form a public, unified agreement from a diversity of personal preferences, beliefs, and opinions. Reasonable discussion and mutual concession are the main tactics of this method. Thus, compromise is related to the Stoic-Roman idea of consensus; its purpose is to facilitate consensus, or rational agreement.

Like consensus, compromise is not a method of perfection, but rather it has as its goal improvement and progress. Such a goal connects it directly with the rational ideal of openness. Compromise cannot be used to determine infallible solutions, or to provide an opportunity for everyone to get exactly what he wants, or to pursue absolutism in any form. Compromise is used to seek workable solutions to matters that must be resolved if life is to continue harmoniously, or even continue at all. Thus, its purpose is to keep democracy going.

This is not to say that compromise is a vulgar condescension from truth, as it is commonly suggested today, or that it stands for an acceptance of less than the best. Until compromises are made, until discussion and concessions have taken place between men who have competing ideas of the good, the best goals for democracy are unknown. It is more to the point to say that a compromise is a gain, for its use carries a society further toward progress, at the same time bringing about respect for democratic values, than can any principle of an absolute sort. Similarly, compromises cannot be forced; they are not ends in themselves. T. V. Smith has said that the limits of compromise are necessity, peace, and progress (pp. 64–80). To the usual meanings of these terms may be added the democratic conviction that compromises are necessary because truth is never final and the good is never absolute, and therefore a method that maintains democratic openness is necessary.

Democratic compromises—reasonable discussion and mutual concession—rely on two conditions: empirical evidence and a scientific analysis of evidence. The conditions of compromise are the facts of experience and the order, test, and evaluation of those facts through reason. Through the scientific method, which is the application of reason to experience, general and systematic knowledge can be formed and made the basis of policy and action. Evidence for and against various compromises or proposals for action is organized, verified, and tested through the scientific method; from this the democrat can decide if a particular compromise is viable, if it works toward or away from democratic ends, if it should be accepted or rejected. In addition to their utility in the democratic process, the conditions of compromise imply democratic values in themselves. A compromise should draw on many sources of evidence, which is a kind of pluralism; that evidence is analyzed through reason, the essential ingredient of the democratic idea; and the evidence and its analysis imply public scrutiny, which is an aspect of the ideal of openness.

Other things have a bearing on the empirical and scientific parts of the democratic methodology—for instance, rules of logic and repeatability in testing. Three more general features are outstanding, though, and must be mentioned, by way of summary, as especially valuable attributes of the democratic methodology: publicity, objectivity, and self-correctability, all of them aspects of the ideal of openness. Publicity implies that the method is open to the scrutiny and use of all who have the right and obligation to make democratic decisions. It implies, too, that plural sources of evidence must be cultivated and, especially for education, that a variety of experience is essential, for it is from this that improvement and progress follow. Objectivity implies not a metaphysical but a procedural concern. The democratic method is employed without partiality to a special substantive point of view and without predetermined results. Self-correctability implies, among other things, that the democratic method recognizes no products as absolute and no ideas as perfect, and the method itself contains an ingredient for review, re-analysis, and change. Taken together, the features of publicity, objectivity, and self-correctability all suggest that use of the democratic method means seeking improvement and progress in the conditions of free men.

In its time Stoicism employed a methodology which is similar in significant respects to democratic methodology. A theory of "consensus" has been mentioned in this connection. Consensus, the agreement of rational men, is a practical method that grew out of the Stoic theory of natural law. Roman philosophers and legal thinkers were instrumental in developing this method for determining policy and action that tend toward the ideal. Stoic consensus, however, like democratic compromise (the purpose of which is to facilitate consensus), is supported by other conditions. To the Stoics, the primary fact of philosophy is life itself; they are concerned first with the fact of existence and with ways in which that existence can be lived well. The Stoics believe that all existence is physical, or material, and, consequently, that all knowledge originates with observed facts and events, that is, through the senses or through experience (D.L. vii. 52).

Experience itself, however, is not a satisfactory guide, for one's perception or interpretation of experience may be erroneous. For instance, a road at a distance appears to narrow into nothingness, but it is found to be in its normal dimension when one approaches the far point. But at that point if one were to look behind him, the road again would appear to be narrowed in the opposite direction. One might get into trouble if he acted on such perceptions. Consequently, the early Stoics sought a criterion by which sense experience could be judged absolutely, that is, without error.

It is the Stoic belief that men err not because their senses are faulty but because they are hasty when judging the evidence the senses present. Diogenes Laertius notes that "over-hastiness in assertion affects the actual course of events, so that, unless we have our perceptions well trained, we are liable to fall into unseemly conduct and heedlessness" (vii. 48). Consequently, if men are to escape error, judgment must be perfected through reason. Epictetus says that when one perceives ignorance, he should "henceforth study no other subject and . . . give heed to no other matter than . . . the criterion of what is in accordance with nature . . . [and] apply that criterion and thus determine each special case" (*Disc.* i. 11. 14–15). Epictetus goes on to agree with the early Stoics that the mind contains "inborn ideas" that are so forceful their truth cannot be doubted, and these ideas are the criteria for judging experience. He gives examples of such ideas: "Who has come into being without an innate concept of what is good and evil, honourable and base, appropriate and inappropriate, and happiness, and of what is proper and falls to our lot, and what we ought to do and what we ought not to do?" (*Disc.* ii. 11. 3–4).

But notice that these are moral ideas. Judgments about the physical world have to be shaped through education. Again Epictetus says, "We come into being without any innate concept of a right-angled triangle, or of a half-tone musical interval, but by a certain systematic method of instruction we are taught the meaning of each of these things, and for that reason those who do not know them also do not fancy that they do" (*Disc.* ii. 11. 2–3). So if the person who believes that a road in fact narrows in the distance were to understand that it is natural for the eye to perceive things at a distance in a different way than things close by (more natural than it is for roads either to vary greatly in dimensions or to indicate a path from one point to another, as they do, and yet not reach the second point because they narrow out of existence), he would not err and base action on his faulty judgment.

But even though the Stoics claim moral certainty through "inborn ideas," more often than not it is impossible for them to act on this basis. Reason might lead one to withhold assent from objectively certain perceptions or to agree to false perceptions on good grounds. Epictetus recognizes this when he says that no man willfully agrees with that which is false, for it is against nature to do so, but at times the false seems to be true (*Disc.* i. 28. 1–2). A story is told about Sphaerus, a student of Zeno and Cleanthes, who was fooled one day by King Ptolemy Philopator when the latter ordered wax pomegranates for the table. Sphaerus was taken in and was about to eat the fruit, when the king exclaimed that he had assented to a false presentation (D.L. vii. 177).

It follows that "inborn ideas" (that is, "certainty") cannot be trusted implicitly, and the Stoic theory has to be amended if it is to be useful in the practical determinations of the true and the false. Sextus Empiricus tells that the Stoics added to their theory the criterion that "no objection must arise" (*Adv. math.* vii. 253). One must not agree to the truth of a perception, no matter how vivid or persuasive it is, until it has been examined from all sides and can withstand all reasonable objections. In practice, this criterion forces the Stoics to resort to a theory of probability if they are to construct knowledge from experience (and, from that, rules of action—moral principles). Every man, but especially the ordinary man, has to judge the probability of evidence if he is to evaluate experience adequately.

Ptolemy Philopator's charge that Sphaerus had assented to a false presentation was rebutted when Sphaerus defined the grounds on which he had assented: "I assented not to the proposition that they are pomegranates, but to another, that there are good grounds for thinking them to be pomegranates. Certainty of presentation and reasonable probability are two totally different things" (D.L. vii. 177).

By turning to probability as a practical guide for life, the Stoics also turn to a form of scientific method in order to evaluate evidence and formulate proposals for action. They use the term "science" generally to denote certain, unerring knowledge (D.L. vii. 163) or to suggest, as Arnold relates (p. 140), the combination of all knowledge into a comprehensive, nonconflicting system. These, however, are not the uses of science to which the Stoic turns when evaluating the details of life, or practical experience, for science of this kind has the function only of an ideal. For the practical judgment of experience, the Stoic uses a form of the scientific method in a way similar to that described in the discussion of the democratic method.

The Stoic's judgment of such things as impressions, opinions, programs, and practicality comes through an examination of the best evidence for and against them. Such an examination leads to judging the consistency and correspondence of perceptions with already accepted knowledge. If a perception is to be accepted as cognitive, or if a theory is to be accepted as the basis of action, it must be judged in relation to other impressions and theories that have been accepted (or rejected) on the same basis. (Christensen, pp. 61, 93n8B, has a good discussion of this method.) It is in this sense that consensus implies rational agreement: the body of intelligent, reflective persons establishes that the best evidence validates or invalidates the truth or worth of a perception or policy. As with the method of science (as it has been shown for both democracy and Stoicism), this does not mean that practical judgments are true for all time. They are, rather, necessary and acceptable formulations within the limits of reason, but they are open to criticism and change whenever experience and reason suggest such a warrant.

Some critics, Edelstein (p. ix), for example, recognize that in its subjective tendencies Stoicism is closer to modern thought than are the classical philosophies of Plato and Aristotle. Perhaps, too, Stoicism is closer to modern thought in its recognition that life is the first and important matter of philosophy and in the fervor with which it communicated its moral message. Stoicism resembles modern existentialism in these particulars, and one may be struck by the existential tone that runs through much Stoic writing—for example, the *Discourses* of Epictetus. An even more striking connection with another kind of modern thought—scientific thought—is the likeness between the practical method by which the Stoics determine truth and the method which is involved in making democratic decisions. Both are methods of reason—discussion, compromise, and consensus. An approach to the ideals of each system is made through a similar application of empiricism and scientific analysis, and the intelligent person acts on the probable determinations of this method. These methods are well chosen to lead men by rational sight, not blind faith, toward the human ideals each represents.

4

Education

PHILOSOPHIC and political theorists must cultivate a distinctive pattern of education if their theories are to prosper. In a general way, such theories are perhaps educational in themselves. John Dewey (p. 328) once defined philosophy as the general theory of education, by which he meant that philosophy and education alike seek to form general intellectual and emotional attitudes toward nature and fellow men. The connection between philosophy and education can be traced from the beginning of Western thought. It can be seen clearly in the work of such philosophers as Plato and Aristotle, but it is also evident in other schools of thought. It is not an overstatement to say that to the Stoics philosophy is wholly a matter of education. Perhaps this is why Epictetus, for example, treats the topics of reason, study, and true freedom so extensively. And, because philosophy is a matter of education, the philosopher is the educator of mankind. Seneca says, "Aristo of Chios . . . limited the 'moral' . . . for he abolished that heading which embraced advice, maintaining that it was the business of pedagogue, not of the philosopher—as if the wise man were anything else than the pedagogue of the human race!" (*Epis.* 89. 13).

Political theory also can be seen as educational theory, either through a philosophic connection or in a direct way. Epictetus relates the two theories in the first way. A criticism made regularly of the Stoics is that they do not become involved in politics, so the state and mankind suffer; Epictetus suggests a more general view of politics: "If you will, ask me also if he is to be active in politics. You ninny, are you looking for any nobler politics than that in which he is engaged? Or would you have someone in Athens step forward and discourse about incomes and revenues, when he is the person who ought to talk with all men, Athenians, Corinthians, and Romans alike, but about happiness and unhappiness, about success and failure, about slavery and freedom? When a man is engaging in such exalted politics, do *you* ask me if he is to engage in politics? Ask me also, if he will hold office. Again I will tell you: Fool, what nobler office will he hold than that which he now has?" (*Disc*. iii. 22. 83–85). From this context, and because philosophy is educational, it follows that politics, too, is educational.

Political theory has an even more direct connection with educational theory. Like philosophy, political theory originated from the direct pressure of educational matters. This connection may also be traced to the beginning of Western thought. The important purpose of political theory is to initiate the citizen into the life of the community, and government exists, in part at least, as an educational institution to perform this task. The work of Sir Ernest Barker makes this point clearly. He says that "the theory of education is essentially a part of political theory" (p. 192). He goes on to say that the Greek educational tradition involves more than such matters as the psychology of learning and teaching (though these things do enter into the theory of education and are important). The theory of education generally is social theory; it is the grasp and comprehension of the purposes, character, and needs of society and state and a discovery of the best methods by which the young can be trained to achieve those purposes, to maintain and improve that character, and to satisfy those needs.

These connections suggest in addition that the original conception and primary purpose of education is moral. Somehow, perhaps because of the increased complexity of life, the interest in specialization and technology, and a heightened concern with educational pedagogy, the moral character of education has been forgotten in modern times (though an interest is being revived presently). Education is more than formal pedagogy, however, and it seeks to unify experience as well as encourage specialization. True education still has the moral aim of producing a man who is capable of doing his duty within the community, an aim identical with the purposes of both Stoicism and democracy. This aim permits a distinction between two types of education: one may be called "training," the kind of education more appropriate to totalitarian societies; the other is education in a more general sense, or education for "understanding," in order to cultivate an ability to comprehend and judge for oneself through reason. Free systems such as democracy and Stoicism are based on the latter kind.

Perhaps in a free society or system of thought, education is even more crucial than in those that are not free; the latter can thrive on general ignorance (or on mere technical ability), but free systems are ruined by ignorance. Thomas Jefferson understood this in the early days of the United States' national experience; his observation that a civilized nation cannot expect to remain both free and ignorant is still a leading challenge for education. Jefferson had read the Greek philosophers, and he must have been aware that the incompatibility of ignorance and freedom, or, positively, the necessity of education for freedom, was recognized also in antiquity. Epictetus implies the same thing when he says that "law is not simply anything that is in the power of a fool" (Disc. iv. 7. 34). Freedom is gained and held through education.

Because of these considerations, it is appropriate to note some educational ideas that evolve from or have a bearing on the analysis presented of the democratic and Stoic theories. The main purpose is to present some Stoic ideas about education. But these ideas also give further evidence for the intellectual connection between democracy and Stoicism and for the belief that in both theories freedom, reason, and education are related.

John E. Rexine, a contributor to a recent volume of essays in the history of education, discusses Stoicism as an educational philosophy by studying Zeno of Citium, the founder of Stoicism (pp. 79–94). This is a perplexing choice. Zeno formulated the original principles of Stoicism, but very little remains today of his own writing and work. This is true also for other early Stoics, Cleanthes and Chrysippus, and even for Panaetius and Posidonius in a later period. What is known of these Stoics comes mostly from fragments collected by commentators on the philosophy. There is reason to believe that Zeno and his followers taught their philosophy with considerable moral fervor and pedagogical skill, but a discussion of their teaching must be, at best, a composite picture (which certainly is the intent of Rexine's essay). Perhaps it is because of the lack of primary sources that few studies have been made of Stoic educational theory. Rexine suggests that Stoic education would include study within the general divisions of philosophy, i.e., logic, physics, and ethics, for the Stoics believed that all knowledge falls within one or another of them, and he recounts some details of early Stoic thinking within each of these divisions. But a different approach might be more fruitful for the study of Stoicism as an educational theory.

There is another who perhaps is a better representative of Stoicism in the history of education: Epictetus. A considerable record remains of Epictetus' lectures and scattered sayings, and that record contains an extensive treatment of educational topics. Epictetus understands that his philosophy, like any moral philosophy, is basically educational. He says, "God counselled Socrates to take the office of examining and confuting men, Diogenes the office of rebuking men in a kingly manner, and Zeno that of instructing men and laying down doctrines" (*Disc.* iii. 21. 20–21). Furthermore, virtue can be taught (*Disc.* ii. 19. 32); his lectures make it plain that the extension of morality is the primary task of education. The Stoic ideal implies the role of teacher; one must not be content to attain virtue, but he must teach others about virtue (*Disc.* iii. 22; Hijmans, p. 20). Epictetus' writings also contain some useful insights into the psychology and pedagogy of teaching and learning. According to Albert Salomon, "In the *Discourses* [Epictetus] presents the unique individuality of the philosopher and of his applied moral method in living contact with various students in concrete situations. Epictetus as teacher anticipates very modern educational methods in his regard for the structure of situations and the changing perspectives in human relationships."

Consequently, the work of Epictetus is the primary source for the following discussion of Stoic education. About this work, W. A. Oldfather, a translator of Epictetus, observes, "We have . . . in [the] *Discourses* a work which . . . is really unique in literature, the actual words of an extraordinarily gifted teacher upon scores, not to say hundreds, of occasions in his own classroom, conversing with visitors, reproving, exhorting, encouraging his pupils, enlivening the dullness of the formal instruction, and, in his own parable, shooting it through with the red stripe of a conscious moral purpose in preparation for the problem of right living" (pp. xiii–xiv). Oldfather concludes that "in view of the singularly valuable nature of the material it seems strange that more attention has not been paid to Epictetus in the history of ancient education" (p. xiv*n*1). (Since the time of these observations, Hijmans has produced a useful book of notes on Epictetus' educational system.) From Epictetus (supported by a few other Stoics, mainly Seneca), the moral aim of a Stoic educational theory and some practical considerations necessary for the achievement of that aim can be clarified. The educational aims and practices of Stoicism are similar to those necessitated by democratic theory, that is, the discussion of educational theory has equal bearing on the formulated theories of Stoicism and democracy.

Freedom is the ideal or the aim of Stoic education. Epictetus says, "We should not trust the multitude, who say, 'Only the free can be educated,' but rather the philosophers who say, 'Only the educated are free' " (*Disc.* ii. 1. 23). By this he does not mean that political freedom is unimportant. Sometimes political freedom itself is a condition for other kinds of freedom (this lesson has been taught most recently in the United States civil rights movement), and a close reading of Epictetus' lectures suggests that he was aware of the value of political freedom. In the *Discourses*, Epictetus tells how Roman soldiers spy and how those who tell their secrets in an unguarded moment may be arrested and imprisoned (iv. 13. 5). He cautions the individual to hold his tongue. "Freedom" in the widest sense means the power to do as one wills, or the power of independent action (*Disc.* ii. 1. 24; D.L., vii. 122), and political freedom certainly is a part of that definition.

With his recognition of the relationship between freedom and education, Epictetus aims to show two things that are important even today: that education must not be a privilege only of those who enjoy a favored status in the community, and that those who have political freedom without freedom of intelligence have something of which they are uncertain, both in meaning and durability. All men need to be educated, for it is education that leads to understanding or knowledge, and this is the basis for any real freedom. The alternative to education is the rule of force, which destroys freedom. Epictetus declares that men should be ruled by reason, not by the cudgel; they should be taught, but not forced (*Disc.* iii. 7. 31–36). He tells a story about Lycurgus (*Frag.* 5), in order to demonstrate that education has better effects than force, and those effects are the beginnings of freedom: "What man among us does not admire the saying of Lycurgus the Lacedaemonian? For when he had been blinded in one eye by one of his fellow-citizens, and the people had turned over the young man to him, to take whatever vengeance upon the culprit he might desire, this he refrained from doing, but brought him up and made a good man of him, and presented him in the theatre. And when the Lacedaemonians expressed their surprise, he said, 'This man when I received him at your hands was insolent and violent; I am returning him to you a reasonable and public-spirited person.' "

Throughout Epictetus' work, and the works of the Stoics in general, there is the belief that error is involuntary. Epictetus says, "What is your idea? That I intentionally fall into evil and miss the good? Far from it! What, then, is the cause of my going astray? Ignorance" (*Disc.* i. 26. 7). One might disagree, but this does serve as a recommendation for education; perhaps a similar recommendation—the belief that most persons, if they are aware of the relative value of intelligence, will choose to act on that basis—is necessary even for modern education. The Stoics believe that ignorance is the lack of proper understanding, which, with an impulsive will, leads to bad judgment and then to error.

Consequently, the principal task of education is to perfect the judgment and reform the will. Epictetus says of the ignorant, "Only show them their error and you will see how quickly they will desist from their mistakes" (*Disc.* i. 18. 3–4). How this perfection can be accomplished is outlined as the Stoic methodology; it is their epistemology. To perfect judgment and control the will, one must understand physical and logical matters. Physical study provides a knowledge of the facts of existence, and logical study is necessary to organize those facts and deduce from them correct judgments and appropriate courses of action.

What must not be overlooked, however, is the fact that education is a moral enterprise, and it must deal ultimately with moral issues and lead to moral ends. The maxim "know thyself," a Greek educational ideal for at least six centuries before his time, is also an ideal for Epictetus (*Disc.* i. 18. 17–18). This maxim is also an ideal for modern education. Existential philosophers especially would think that it expresses succinctly the real aim of education. Ludwig Edelstein describes this educational ideal, from the Stoic point of view, in terms of modern philosophy: "Man is able to rise from the level of unauthentic existence to that of authentic existence, from fraudulent being to true being; and we do this when we understand who we are in reality and decide to be what we are" (p. 38).

According to the Stoics, a person needs education so that he will know how to conform to nature and thus be happy and live wisely. Consequently, Epictetus deplores the overemphasis given to studies that do not deal directly with moral topics. He says, "Let others practice lawsuits, others problems, others syllogisms; do you practice how to die, how to be enchained, how to be racked, how to be exiled" (*Disc*. ii. 1. 38–39). The intent here is not to argue that logic can be overlooked. An understanding of logic is basic to morality. Epictetus notes that without logic one cannot even learn if that study itself is necessary (*Disc*. ii. 25). He also disapproves of literary achievement (*Disc*. ii. 17. 35–36); but, as Hijmans points out, it is the kind of literary achievement that should have been attained earlier, or which is an end in itself, and which interferes with moral education (p. 35).

Sometimes men mistake particular studies, as important as they are, for the real aim of education, in the same way that they mistake the wise man's appearance for wisdom itself (Epictetus, *Disc*. i. 8. 11–16; iv. 8. 1–9). That is, sometimes the process of education gets in its own way, and the ends toward which one is working are obscured. Studies then become ends in themselves, or they are followed for the popular appearance of education; and their relationship to something more important, to the moral life, is forgotten. It is this tendency that Epictetus deplores: "When I speak thus to some people they think that I am disparaging the study. . . . Yet I am not disparaging this, but only the habit of dwelling unceasingly on these matters and setting one's hopes in them" (*Disc*. ii. 23. 46).

Examples of other studies can illustrate the primary importance of moral education and show how all studies must contribute to that end. The significance of another branch of logic, the definition of terms, must not be overlooked: whoever attempts the task of education "ought to understand the meaning of terms. . . . Use is one thing, and understanding another" (Epictetus, *Disc*. ii. 14. 14–16). Sometimes, though, this study, like other studies, becomes an end in itself, or it is used to confuse rather than clarify or to gain a popular victory over good sense. This will not happen if the moral consequences that stem from improper attention to the study are kept in mind: "Indeed, to sum up the whole matter," Epictetus says, "if all of us who have these terms upon our lips possess no mere empty knowledge of each one severally, and do not need to devote any pains to the systematic arrangement of our preconceived ideas, why do we disagree, why fight, why blame one another?" (Disc. ii. 17. 13).

Reading and speaking also are necessary studies, but they too must be used correctly. Reading is easier when writing is plain, and listening is easier when language is plain, Epictetus says (Disc. ii. 23. 1), so it is important to study the faculty of expression. However, the proper object of reading and speaking is to deal with impressions when action is necessary; and unless reading and speaking lead to peace of mind, Epictetus questions the use of such study (Disc. iv. 4. 1–5; iii. 23).

Some educational principles may be formulated from these observations. First, education has a moral aim and studies must be oriented to that aim, a point already made. Second, though some educational matters have higher priority than others, one must not neglect the others. Epictetus remarks about this for the faculties, but it is true also of subjects to be studied and the relationship of studies to the ends of education. He says, "Yet because some things are superior we ought not to despise the use which the others give. There is a certain value also in the faculty of eloquence, but it is not as great as that of the faculty of moral purpose. When, therefore, I say this, let no one suppose that I am bidding you neglect speech, any more than I bid you neglect eyes, or ears, or hands, or feet, or dress, or shoes" (Disc. ii. 23. 25–27). Third, accidental qualities must not be confused with the real marks of intelligence and education. Confusion of this kind is most often based on physical characteristics, clothes, or popularity; but the point refers also to a confusion between the appearance of study and the end of study.

Finally, there is the idea that education must be direct and purposeful. This is a chief principle that can be taken from the preceding discussion; unfortunately, it is not followed readily even in modern times. Epictetus believes that if one is to gain a certain end, he must not work toward another (*Disc.* iii. 6. 1–4). Thus, because the true aim of education is a moral one, we must deal with moral topics if that aim is·to be achieved, and studies that make only a partial contribution to morality must not be overemphasized. The failure to follow this principle is given by Epictetus to explain why modern man makes less moral progress than did the ancients (*Disc.* iii. 6. 1–4). Seneca also implied that education must be direct and purposeful in his criticism of reading: "You complain that in your part of the world there is a scant supply of books. But it is quality, rather than quantity, that matters; a limited list of reading benefits; a varied assortment serves only for delight. He who would arrive at the appointed end must follow a single road and not wander through many ways. What you suggest is not travelling; it is mere tramping" (*Epis.* 45. 1).

Seneca's statement should not be misunderstood. It should not be taken to mean that the end of education—intelligence, truth, freedom—can be gained absolutely or that only one road leads to that end. A theory of education based on such an opinion would stifle rather than liberate, and it would contradict the ideal of openness discussed earlier. The statement is intended to convey the point that the process of education, or the search for truth, must not be hindered by unimportant matters. This point is clarified by Seneca in another statement: "Whatever the quality of my works may be, read them as if I were still seeking, and were not aware of, the truth, and were seeking it obstinately, too. For I have sold myself to no man; I bear the name of no master. I give much credit to the judgment of great men; but I claim something also for my own. For these men, too, have left to us, not positive discoveries, but problems whose solution is still to be sought. They might perhaps have discovered the essentials, had they not sought the superfluous also" (*Epis.* 45. 4).

At the same time there is an indication in this point of view that something new always can be gained through education, that education is an endless process. We have seen that Seneca believed that men who have advanced the cause of truth should be followed as guides, not masters; the truth is open to everyone; it has not been monopolized, and plenty is left for future discovery (*Epis.* 33. 11). Also, he says in another place, "Much still remains to do, and much will always remain, and he who shall be born a thousand years hence will not be barred from his opportunity of adding something further" (*Epis.* 64. 7).

A general Stoic opinion is reflected in this last observation. Seneca is not alone among the Stoics in the belief that education is a continual process. The belief implies that the process of education must not be blocked, especially by the conviction that one already has the truth. Epictetus observes that one cannot learn what he thinks he knows already (*Disc.* ii. 17. 1), and this belief is central to Stoic educational thought. For instance, the school has learning as its purpose, to correct opinions or to exchange them, not to keep the same ones (*Disc.* ii. 21. 15–17). Epictetus asks rhetorically, "What do we go to the philosophers for? To learn what we do *not* think we know" (*Disc.* ii. 17. 3). In other places, he says that learning cannot take place as long as men are hardened in argument or are deaf and blind to their faults; such people cannot be reasoned with (*Disc.* i. 5; ii. 20. 37). Consequently, one must be open to learning. Socrates is used as an example by Epictetus: "Just as Socrates used to tell us not to live a life unsubjected to examination, so we ought not to accept a sense-impression unsubjected to examination, but should say, 'Wait, allow me to see who you are and whence you come' (just as the night-watch say, 'Show me your tokens')" (*Disc.* iii. 12. 15).

But even Stoic examples must not be followed uncritically, for great men may be wrong at times. Epictetus admits that even Homer is not an authority in everything (*Disc.* iii. 24. 18). One who slavishly follows examples fails to see the important point that wise men demonstrate—that one must examine things for oneself and form one's own judgments. According to Epictetus, it is a law of nature that "if you wish any good thing, get it from yourself" (*Disc.* i. 29. 4). It follows from these observations that education cannot be effective if one believes that what he already knows is good enough. Rather, the wise person is open always to new possibilities and can see something that still needs to be done. Perhaps "the cures for the spirit also have been discovered by the ancients," Seneca says; still, at least "it is our task to learn the method and the time of treatment" (*Epis.* 64. 8).

Some similarities can now be drawn between Stoic education and the kind of education necessary in a democracy. The similarities most likely appear in all free systems of thought. It has been noted that both Stoicism and democracy follow the ideal of openness. For education, this means essentially that, if one is to learn (in order to be free), he must not act as if the truth is known already or that what is known is good enough. Thus, in effect, free education is a challenge to absolutism. Boyd Bode says this is true for democracy: "A democratic program of education must necessarily rest on the perception that democracy is a challenge to all forms of absolutism . . ." (*Progressive Education*, p. 39). It can be concluded from Stoic opinion presented that it is true also for Stoicism.

Also, in free systems, education is a process of self-development. The individual must play a major role in his own education, and the process of education is the search for his own being, meaning, and worth. For this reason, indoctrination, or the teaching of a partisan point of view exclusively, is neither the aim nor the method of a free education. The Stoics are clear in their recommendation that it is insufficient to follow the advice of others; one must examine things for himself. For democracy, H. Gordon Hullfish believes, "indoctrination is not an appropriate act. . . . Conformity is not an appropriate goal" (p. 11), because indoctrination and conformity destroy the individual. For the student particularly, indoctrination begins as a necessity to follow another's ideas uncritically, and it leads to a conformity where there remains no ability to be critical. In this pattern the student does not think for himself, cannot act on his own thinking, and cannot be responsible for his own life. Thus, freedom is contradicted.

Where indoctrination and conformity are found, however, they are not always the marks of a deliberate attempt to deny freedom. Sometimes these practices arise from the belief that all forms of education must set out specific methods or programs that can be followed universally. This is a mistaken belief; nevertheless, it is popular in that it is both widespread and easily formulated. But Hullfish is correct when he says that democratic education "does not lead us to a series of methods that each teacher may use in the same way nor to a set of curriculum or administrative devices of universal applicability" (p. 14). The mistaken belief that educational theories can recommend specific programs of universal application is similar to the mistake made by those who confuse an intellectual approach or a general method, such as the method of reason or the scientific method, with particular beliefs, programs, or answers. A free educational theory is a general theory, from which specific methods or programs depend in great part on the context—the time and place, the individuals involved, the consequences to be considered, and so on.

For this reason it is perplexing to note that some persons criticize general theories of education for not dealing with specific things. An example that may apply to both democracy and Stoicism is the criticism that Phillip DeLacy makes of the Stoic system, in a review of Georges Pire's book, *Stoicisme et Pedagogie*. DeLacy believes there is "a curious paradox" in the relation of Stoic education to life. Education, which is the perfection of reason, is a preparation for life; but, DeLacy says, since reason is the only true good, Stoic education has very little to say about the specific things to be pursued or avoided (p. 334). Unless DeLacy means that Stoic educational theory should "suggest" specific action to be taken, which any educational theory might do through examples or precepts, and should be used as a guide for teaching and learning, it is ill conceived to think that it could do so in any more necessary way.

The writings of Epictetus contain a wealth of "suggestions" for education. These range from psychological insights about the nature and process of teaching and learning to very specific matters such as the relationship of good grooming and proper speech to the end of moral education. Beyond this, however, Epictetus is well aware that the student cannot be told what to do. It is easy, perhaps too easy, to follow the dominant doctrine of a school; the insistent appeal of students, even today, for specific and detailed directions bears this out. Hijmans reminds the student (p. 10) that Epictetus believes that the inner acceptance of the general principles of moral education makes specific instructions superfluous (*Disc.* iv. 1. 51). That is, to ask for specific instructions is a clear indication that the general principles of education have not been grasped.

Hijmans notes further that such instructions are difficult to give, even when the student insists on them (p. 94). It is impossible to describe techniques which in the nature of things are adaptable to various persons and circumstances. The circumstantial quality of life is recognized by Epictetus. In a part of his work that comes close to suggesting specific things to be obeyed or shunned, he says, nevertheless, of oath-taking, "Refuse, if you can, to take an oath at all, but if that is impossible, refuse as far as circumstances allow" (*Man.* 33). Finally, to determine one's own education is to pursue freedom. What Seneca says about the learning of precepts is an example for education in general: "We [Stoics] allow the purchasers themselves to get their samples from anywhere they please. . . . We Stoics are not subjects of a despot: each of us lays claim to his own freedom" (*Epis.* 33. 3–4).

The emphasis on self-education should not conflict with the idea of social growth. In democracy and in Stoicism, the individual is responsible for his own life and education; in part this is what it means to be free. But responsibility implies a social context; one's individualism relates to others. In education, the individual interacts with others in numerous ways: in the usual student-teacher relationships, in discussions, by using others as examples (good and bad), and through an understanding of history or the evolution of human progress. Possession of education implies a context within which one becomes conscious of himself and society. It suggests further that the special purpose of education is to clarify the meaning of the society within which it operates—the characteristics, purposes, achievements, and shortcomings—and to challenge the student to conceive and carry out a unique role in such a society. Self-education is not education in isolation but rather a social education that leads to a perception of a role one can play in the world.

Similarly, democratic education implies a continuous process. Such a thing follows from the ideal of openness that guides the general theory of democracy, and it is like the continuous process implied in Stoicism and Stoic education. No reasoning about such a process for democratic education is more to the point than John Dewey's discussion of education as growth. According to Dewey (chap. 4), growth is a potentiality that is positive and intrinsic; it is the ability of a thing to develop for an end, and that end is nothing other than itself. One can say, for example, that the aim of an individual is to develop for himself and the aim of democracy is to develop for itself. The actual process of growth, in which development is made, is education.

It follows that education is its own end. This means that democratic education must serve continuously to widen the perspective of democratic participants. Dewey says, "The educational process is one of continual reorganizing, reconstructing, transforming" (p. 50). The task is the one mentioned: through education one clarifies and deepens his understanding of democracy. At the same time, there is no end to this process—no final meaning of democracy. Thus, the growth that comes through democratic education is a form of improvement, not perfection. Democratic education aims specifically for improved intelligence, which in turn is used to improve the conditions of life. In these ways, democratic and Stoic forms of education agree.

Other Stoic topics have implications for education. In the study of these topics one is impressed repeatedly with the fact that Stoic education is essentially a matter of self-responsibility and effort, and the aim of education is individual freedom and, through the unity of mankind, the well-being of society. Epictetus announces a common Stoic opinion: "no one comes to his fall because of another's deed" (*Disc.* i. 28. 23). The reason men generally do not employ intelligence to control their lives, Seneca says, is that they are unwilling, though always the excuse is inability (*Epis.* 117. 8). Consequently, it is necessary to motivate the student, to challenge him to give education a try. This is what Epictetus says: "Let us let bygones be bygones. Only let us begin, and, take my word for it, you shall see" (*Disc.* ii. 19. 34); "And that you may learn the truth of all this, as you have toiled for those other things, so also transfer your toil to these. . . . Anyway, try it at least; there is no disgrace in making the attempt" (*Disc.* iv. 1. 176–77). This motivation, of course, comes from the teacher, but its effectiveness depends on the student also. Epictetus observes that if students were eager and willing to learn instead of playing, it would be much easier for the older person, especially the teacher, to take his studies seriously (*Disc.* i. 10. 13).

The student can help prepare himself for education by understanding that learning requires attention and diligence. Education is a difficult process, but, Epictetus says, difficulties show men's character (*Disc.* i. 24. 1). In their own instruction, the Stoics employ examples of men like Hercules who overcame great difficulty and are admired for it. Difficulty can be overcome through education, but Epictetus does not suggest that the work can be mastered

quickly or will have universal results. The principal doctrines of philosophy are brief, he says, but it is no brief
study that enables one to learn those doctrines (*Disc.* i.
20. 14–16; i. 15). Seneca also knows that education is not
a short-term project, for man is ignorant in some respects
all his life: "You should keep learning as long as you are
ignorant,—even to the end of your life, if there is anything
in the proverb" (*Epis.* 76. 3). Nevertheless, persistent attention or diligence is worthwhile. It may be impossible to
escape error altogether, Epictetus says (*Disc.* iv. 12. 19), but
it is possible to set the mind toward consistently avoiding
errors, and this matter is worth persistence even if one
escapes only a few errors.

The Stoics put the greatest educational emphasis on practice. This is consistent with their "active" philosophy. Stoic
physics is an active materialism; their logic is a theory of
active intelligence; and these studies support an active ethi-
cal theory, or a theory of conduct designed as an actual
guide for human affairs. Education itself is part of the active
ethics, so it must emphasize practice. Education can show
why practice is necessary, how it can be accomplished,
and what consequences follow from practice or the lack
of practice. Furthermore, it is through practice that the
student becomes a distinctive, self-responsible, intelligent
individual.

Of course, practice must be intelligent, that is, one must
practice the right thing. Seneca says, " 'What is wisdom?
Always desiring the same things, and always refusing the
same things.' You may be excused from adding the little
proviso,—that what you wish, should be right; since no
man can always be satisfied with the same thing, unless
it is right" (*Epis.* 20. 5). Some persons confuse the aim
of education, which is freedom, with the right to do anything they please. Others confuse commitment to an idea,

or steadfastness, with virtue itself, without inquiring if the idea is right or wrong. These confusions were known to the Stoics, but, sadly enough, they are still made in modern education. Epictetus speaks of these things; his warnings are still appropriate. Freedom is not frenzied volition, Epictetus cautions (*Disc.* i. 12. 9–10); it is not getting whatever one wants, if what one wants is not the right thing. On the other hand, to the person who thought that "I must abide by my decisions," Epictetus gives the qualified reply, "You mean not *all* your decisions, but only the right ones" (*Disc.* ii. 15. 7). It is not that Epictetus wants to dictate what is right for all persons. Each person must make his own decisions and pursue virtue in his own way. Epictetus' aim is to remind the student that freedom is gained only through intelligence. Pure volition and uncritical commitment are a violation of intelligence and can lead to no good. Thus, he says, "Do you not wish . . . to consider whether your decision is sound or unsound, and only after you have done that proceed to rear thereon the structure of your determination and your firm resolve?" (*Disc.* ii. 15. 8).

Once a person is convinced by examination that his principles are right, he must act on those principles. The Stoics believe that a man is not like a stone or a log, that it can be shown what he is by pointing a finger. Epictetus knows, rather, that men are evaluated by what they do, by their judgments, and by the kinds of actions to which their judgments lead (*Disc.* iii. 2). This belief brings other thoughts into focus, such as those relating to the publicity of one's acts, the use of examples and precepts or maxims, and the way in which ability can be proven. One cannot hope to practice the principles of philosophy unseen. Ethics is in fact a social activity; it deals with conduct, which is social, so that it is foolish to think that moral principles can be practiced without the action being seen.

On the contrary, one must be prepared to act on his principles and to have that action observed, but this should hold no fear for the true student. If the observation of one's action leads the student to become aware of his faults and to change them, it is helpful. Even if observation leads to unjust criticism and to social condemnation and unpopularity, Epictetus believes one should not avoid being seen to do his duty if he has determined that it is the proper thing to be done (*Man.* 35). Moreover, one should even take deliberate steps to be seen in association with moral men and in pursuit of virtue. He advises, "Devote yourself to a philosopher instead of to a rich old man, be seen about *his* doors; it will be no disgrace to be so seen, you will not retire thence empty and without profit, if you approach him in the right fashion" (*Disc.* iv. 1. 176–77).

It is good advice that the student should associate with those who have learned—with other students who have made greater progress and with teachers, as well as statesmen, philosophers, and even soldiers who set fine examples of moral conscience for the rest of mankind. Seneca believes that "Nothing is more successful in bringing honourable influences to bear upon the mind, or in straightening out the wavering spirit that is prone to evil, than association with good men" (*Epis.* 94. 40). At times one might go as far to learn the words, or maxims and precepts, of wise men. Such learning has been a part of education for more than two millenia; it is practiced less now than formerly, but it is still practiced. The Stoics, like the Greeks in general, draw maxims and precepts from ancient literature, especially from the poets and dramatists and some of the great philosophers, in order to support their teaching. Some Stoic teachings themselves, such as Epictetus' *Manual*, seem to be intended for use in this way and have been so used throughout history.

Seneca treats the matter of precepts in his *Epistles* (94, 95), and he comes to the conclusion that they are a necessary part of education. Moreover, the student should not hesitate to appropriate for his own use what has been said by others. If the work contributes to virtue, that is, if it aids in the process of becoming educated, it is common property. This is Seneca's meaning when he says, "Whatever is well said by anyone is mine" (*Epis.* 16. 7). Past studies have some bearing on present study; therefore, they should be used for what they are worth. Again Seneca says, "It makes a great deal of difference whether you approach a subject that has been exhausted, or one where the ground has merely been broken; in the latter case, the topic grows day by day, and what is already discovered does not hinder new discoveries. Besides, he who writes last has the best of the bargain; he finds already at hand worlds which, when marshalled in a different way, show a new face. And he is not pilfering them, as if they belonged to someone else, when he uses them, for they are common property" (*Epis.* 79. 6).

Maxims and precepts, however, are not the whole of education, and their study is not to be recommended exclusively or absolutely. This is true also of reading and dialectical argument and similar things. These studies must lead to action; if they do not, they have no value in Stoic education. Both Epictetus (*Disc.* iii. 21) and Seneca (*Epis.* 108. 38–39) note that anyone can talk about what is good and bad and can quote the doctrines of others, but the educated person shows the results of study and training in his own life. Unfortunately, study is not always demonstrated outside the classroom. "The proverb about the Lacedaemonians, 'Lions at home, but at Ephesus foxes,' will fit us too," Epictetus says (*Disc.* iv. 5. 37): "Lions in the school-room, foxes outside." One reason for this is that many people master literary accounts but have no real understanding of them, so that from their study they can form no judgments and actions. Epictetus gives an example (*Frag.* 15): some women of Rome were attracted to Plato's *Republic* because he advocated community of wives. These women looked only at what Plato said, and they did not understand the real meaning, so they could not benefit from his idea.

Mistakes of this kind are made even today. Rexine says that Zeno did not intend to convince people of his doctrines by reason; rather, his sententious maxims were "witticisms" that caught on because of a people's desperate need for something to which they could cling (pp. 90–91). This evaluation is out of character with the life of Zeno, and if it is meant to reflect on the intent of Stoicism in general, it is simply in error. Rexine's misunderstanding is due perhaps to a too simple reading of Zeno's maxims and a failure to understand the place of maxims in Stoic education. The whole intent of Stoicism is to establish reason as a guide for action. The pithy sayings for which Zeno was so well known to his generation must be judged on the basis of whether or not they contribute to the life of reason.

Diogenes Laertius makes it clear that the maxims are intended to teach moral principles, not to be mere lifebuoys or witticisms. He says, "[Zeno] used to say that it was not the words and expressions that we ought to remember, but we should exercise our mind in disposing to advantage of what we hear, instead of, as it were, tasting a well cooked dish or well dressed meal" (D.L. vii. 22). Later Stoics were of the same mind, for according to Seneca, " 'Whom,' you say, 'shall I call upon [for a teacher]? Shall it be this man or that?' There is another choice also open to you; you may go to the ancients; for they have the time to help you. We can get assistance not only from the living, but from those of the past. Let us choose, however, from among the living, not men who pour forth their words with the greatest glibness, burning out commonplaces, and holding, as it were, their own little private exhibitions, not these, I say, but men who teach us by their lives, men who tell us what we ought to do and then are never caught doing that which they have ordered us to avoid" (*Epis.* 52. 7–8).

Seneca's statement suggests also that the teacher has a considerable role in education. This role has been touched on only as it involves examples and advice, but one should not believe from this that the teacher is unimportant. It is true, according to Epictetus (*Disc.* i. 17. 29), that the teacher is not needed for his own sake—neither is any other person—but a good teacher can help the student along the right path of education. This help is so important that Epictetus says men have a right to be angry when the teacher tells them nothing of use (*Frag.* 19). The student should not trust his mind and his education to any chance comer, Epictetus believes, any more than he would trust his body to the first person he meets (*Man.* 28). Thus, teachers who have nothing useful to say and those who cannot teach effectively should not be used. Epictetus notes that some teachers dispense with the student as ignorant instead of realizing their own incapacity to teach (*Disc.* ii. 12. 2). Teaching cannot be done off-hand or in a random fashion. Rather, it demands mature years, a way of life, and guidance by reason; and Epictetus discusses the meaning of these things in considerable detail (*Disc.* iii. 21).

The image of the teacher is a good point from which to summarize Stoic education and to make a final observation about the similarity between Stoicism and democracy. In *The Hero in History* Sidney Hook says that democratic education requires a different ideal than men who make events (pp. 237–38). The heroes of democracy are the great men of thought, of ideas, of social vision, of science and art. They are the teachers who have given the people vision, method, and knowledge. The point of this essay is that the Stoic is such a man. He is a teacher in the finest sense. He takes responsibility for his own life, which he lives through intelligence. At the same time the Stoic is a student, forever seeking knowledge and using it as the basis for action. Stoicism is a challenge to old ways of life. Its aim is freedom, which in the world requires constant reorganization of thought and action. In his own time, and even today, the Stoic stands high as an example of knowledge and virtue. Stoicism and democracy have similar ideals and methods, but equally important, they imply a similar plan of education for describing and promoting their ways of life. Not only is the educated man, the man of reason, the true hero (ideal) of both democracy and Stoicism; he is the only man who is free.

Appendix: Classical Citations

The following abbreviations are used for classical citations:

Cicero	*De finibus*	*Fin.*
	De officiis	*Off.*
	De oratore	*Orat.*
	De republica	*Rep.*
Diogenes Laertius	*Lives*	D.L.
Epictetus	*Discourses*	*Disc.*
	Fragments	*Frag.*
	Manual	*Man.*
Marcus Aurelius	*Meditations*	M.A.
Plutarch	*Lives (Cato the Younger)*	*Cato*
Seneca	*Epistles*	*Epis.*
Sextus Empiricus	*Adversus mathematicos*	*Adv. math.*

Citations are made from the following Loeb Classical Library editions:

Cicero. *De Finibus Bonorum et Malorum.* Translated by H. Rackham. London: William Heinemann, Ltd., 1961. First published in this edition in 1914.

Diogenes Laertius. *Lives of Eminent Philosophers.* Translated by R. D. Hicks. 2 vols. London: William Heinemann, Ltd., 1959 and 1958. First published in this edition in 1925.

Epictetus. *The Discourses as Reported by Arrian*, *The Manual*, *and Fragments*. Translated by W. A. Oldfather. 2 vols. London: William Heinemann, Ltd., 1961. First published in this edition in 1925 and 1928.

Plutarch. *Lives*, vol. 8, *Cato the Younger*. Translated by Bernadotte Perrin. London: William Heinemann, Ltd., 1914–26.

Seneca. *Ad Lucilium Epistulae Morales*. Translated by Richard M. Gummere. 3 vols. London: William Heinemann, Ltd., 1961–62. First published in this edition in 1917, 1920, 1925.

Because the Loeb edition of the *Meditations* of Marcus Aurelius was not available, an Oxford edition has been used: *The Meditations of the Emperor Marcus Antonius*, translated by A. S. L. Farquharson, 2 vols. (Oxford: The Clarendon Press, 1944). Both this and the Loeb editions have facing pages of English and ancient language (Greek or Latin). The very few other classical citations in the text have been taken from Loeb editions when they were available.

Bibliography

Agard, Walter R. *What Democracy Meant to the Greeks*. Chapel Hill: University of North Carolina Press, 1942.

Arnold, E. Vernon. *Roman Stoicism*. London: Routledge & Kegan Paul, Ltd., 1958. First published in 1911.

Baldry, H. C. *The Unity of Mankind in Greek Thought*. Cambridge: At the University Press, 1965.

Barker, Ernest. *Church, State and Education*. Ann Arbor: University of Michigan Press, 1957.

Bayles, Ernest. *Democratic Educational Theory*. New York: Harper and Brothers, 1960.

Becker, Carl L. *Modern Democracy*. New Haven: Yale University Press, 1964. First published in 1941.

Bevan, Edwyn. *Stoics and Sceptics*. Cambridge, England: W. Heffer and Sons, Ltd., 1959. First published in 1913.

Blackham, H. J. *Humanism*. Harmondsworth, England: Penguin Books, Ltd., 1968.

Bode, Boyd H. "Ends and Means in Education, or the Conflicts in Our Cultural Heritage." In *What is Democracy?* edited by Winifred Johnston. Norman, Oklahoma: Cooperative Books, 1939.

————. *Progressive Education at the Crossroads*. New York: Newson & Company, 1938.

Boorstin, Daniel J. *The Genius of American Politics*. Chicago: University of Chicago Press, 1953.

Bryce, Lord James. *Modern Democracies*. Vol. 1. New York: Macmillan Company, 1924.

Castle, E. B. *Ancient Education and Today*. Baltimore: Penguin Books, Inc., 1961.

Christensen, Johnny. *An Essay on the Unity of Stoic Philosophy*. Copenhagen: Munksgaard, 1962.

DeLacy, Phillip. Review of *Stoicisme et Pedagogie*, by Georges Pire. *American Journal of Philology* 80 (July 1959):333–34.

Dewey, John. *Democracy and Education*. New York: Macmillan Company, 1963.

Dobson, J. F. *Ancient Education and Its Meaning to Us*. New York: Cooper Square Publishers, Inc., 1963. First published in 1932.

Dudley, Donald R. "Stoicism and Roman Politics: Introduction and Prospects." *History Today* 13 (November 1963):767–73, 805.

Ebenstein, William. *Today's Isms*. Englewood Cliffs, N.J.: Prentice-Hall, Inc., 1961. First published in 1954.

Edelstein, Ludwig. *The Meaning of Stoicism*. Cambridge: Harvard University Press, 1966.

Frankel, Charles. *The Democratic Prospect*. New York: Harper & Row, Publishers, 1964.

Glover, T. R. *Democracy in the Ancient World*. Cambridge: At the University Press, 1927.

Gould, Josiah B. *The Philosophy of Chrysippus*. Albany: State University of New York Press, 1970.

Grampp, W. D. "Moral Hero and the Economic Man." *Ethics* 61 (January 1951):136–50.

Gummere, Richard M. *Seneca*. Boston: Marshall Jones Company, 1922.

Hadas, Moses. *The Greek Ideal and Its Survival*. New York: Harper & Row, Publishers, Inc., 1966. First published in 1960 as *Humanism: The Greek Ideal and Its Survival*.
————, ed. *The Stoic Philosophy of Seneca*. Garden City, N.Y.: Doubleday & Company, Inc., 1958.
Hallowell, John H. *The Moral Foundations of Democracy*. Chicago: University of Chicago Press, 1954.
Hatch, Edwin. *The Influence of Greek Ideas on Christianity*. New York: Harper & Row, Publishers, Inc., 1957. The Hibbert Lectures, 1888.
Hicks, R. D. *Stoic and Epicurean*. New York: Russell & Russell, Inc., 1962. First published in 1910.
Hijmans, B. L., Jr. *ASKESIS: Notes on Epictetus' Educational System*. Assen, Netherlands: Van Gorcum & Company, N.V., 1959.
Hook, Sidney. *The Hero in History*. Boston: Beacon Press, 1955.
————. "The New Failure of Nerve." In *The Quest for Being*, by Sidney Hook. New York: Dell Publishing Company, Inc., 1963.
Hullfish, H. Gordon. *Toward a Democratic Education*. Columbus: Ohio State University, 1960.
Jaeger, Werner. *Paideia*. Translated by Gilbert Highet. 3 vols. New York: Oxford University Press, 1939–44.
Jones, A. H. M. *Athenian Democracy*. Oxford: B. Blackwell, 1957.
Kennan, George F. *Democracy and the Student Left*. New York: Bantam Books, Inc., 1968.
LeBoutillier, Cornelia G. *American Democracy and Natural Law*. New York: Columbia University Press, 1950.
Marrou, Henri I. *A History of Education in Antiquity*. Translated by George Lamb. New York: The New American Library of World Literature, Inc., 1964. First published in 1948.
Martin, Oliver. "Beyond Compromise." *Ethics* 58 (January 1948):118–22.
Mates, Benson. *Stoic Logic*. Berkeley: University of California Press, 1961. First published in 1953.
Mayo, Henry B. *Introduction to Democratic Theory*. New York: Oxford University Press, 1960.
Merriam, Charles E. *What Is Democracy?* Chicago: University of Chicago Press, 1941.
Millar, Fergus. "Epictetus and the Imperial Court." *Journal of Roman Studies* 55 (1965):141–48.
Murray, Gilbert. *Five Stages of Greek Religion*. Garden City, N.Y.: Doubleday & Company, Inc., 1955. First published in 1912 as *Four States of Greek Religion*.
————. *Humanist Essays*. London: George Allen & Unwin, Ltd., 1964. Contains "The Stoic Philosophy," the Moncure Conway Memorial Lecture of 1915.
————. *The Stoic Philosophy*. New York: G. P. Putnam's Sons, 1915.
Oldfather, W. A., ed. and trans. Introduction to *The Discourses as Reported by Arrian, The Manual, and Fragments*, by Epictetus. Vol. 1. London: William Heinemann, 1961. First published in 1925.
Olson, Robert G. *An Introduction to Existentialism*. New York: Dover Publications, Inc., 1962.
Peirce, Charles S. "The Scientific Attitude and Fallibilism." In *The Philosophy of Peirce: Selected Writings*, edited by Justus Buchler. New York: Harcourt, Brace and Company, 1940.
Pire, Georges. *Stoicisme et Pedagogie*. Paris: Librairie Philosophique, J. Vrin, 1958.
Reesor, Margaret E. *The Political Theory of the Old and Middle Stoa*. New York: J. J. Augustin, 1951.
Rexine, John E. "The Stoic: Zeno." In *The Educated Man; Studies in the History of Educational*

Thought, edited by Paul Nash, Andreas M. Kazamias, and Henry J. Perkinson. New York: John Wiley & Sons, Inc., 1965.

Salomon, Albert. Introduction to *Epictetus: The Enchiridion*. Indianapolis, Indiana: Liberal Arts Press, Inc., 1948.

Sambursky, S. *Physics of the Stoics*. New York: Macmillan Company, 1959.

Saunders, Jason L. *Justus Lipsius: The Philosophy of Renaissance Stoicism*. New York: Liberal Arts Press, 1955.

Simon, Yves R. *The Philosophy of Democratic Government*. Chicago: University of Chicago Press, 1961.

Smith, T. V. *The Ethics of Compromise and the Art of Containment*. Boston: Starr King Press, 1956.

Strauss, Leo. *Natural Right and History*. Chicago: University of Chicago Press, 1953.

Tarn, W. W. *Hellenistic Civilization*. London: Edward Arnold & Company, 1936. First published in 1927.

Thorson, Thomas L. *The Logic of Democracy*. New York: Holt, Rinehart and Winston, 1962.

Tillich, Paul. *The Courage to Be*. New Haven: Yale University Press, 1952.

Watson, Gerard. *The Stoic Theory of Knowledge*. Belfast, N.I.: The Queen's University, 1966.

Wenley, R. M. *Stoicism and Its Influence*. New York: Cooper Square Publishers, Inc., 1963. First published in 1924.

Zeller, Eduard. *The Stoics, Epicureans and Sceptics*. Translated by Oswald J. Reichel. New York: Russell & Russell, Inc., 1962. First published in 1892.

UNIVERSITY OF FLORIDA MONOGRAPHS

Humanities

667339

WITHDRAWN
RITTER LIBRARY
BALDWIN-WALLACE COLLEGE